T0194295

Christians and Courtship

Helping Young People to Live a Dating
in Holiness and with Purpose

César Donaldo Arzú

WESTBOW
PRESS®
A DIVISION OF THOMAS NELSON
& ZONDERVAN

WestBow Press books may be ordered through booksellers or by contacting:

WestBow Press
A Division of Thomas Nelson & Zondervan
1663 Liberty Drive
Bloomington, IN 47403
www.westbowpress.com
1 (866) 928-1240

ISBN: 978-1-9736-5141-3 (sc)
ISBN: 978-1-9736-5142-0 (e)

Print information available on the last page.

WestBow Press rev. date: 01/15/2019

Table of Contents

Special Thanks To

Since the beginning of my Christian faith, I have had as mentors very special people who have done their best effort to transmit to me the Biblical values, so I can put them in practice as life values. Replicate part of those values in other people as well, it is what has driven me to write this book. This is why I take advantage of this space to make a public recognition to those people who are worthy of earthly praise on my behalf and a crown of victory from the Lord who they serve in a willingly way.

Special Thanks to Jorge Alberto Orellana for having the patience to evangelize me for three years and also for teaching me the first steps of a gospel centered in the Bible.

Thanks to pastor Jorge Mario Orellana for inviting me to become part of the founder team of the Central American Evangelist Church "Mies" in Puerto Barrios, in which once installed, he gave me the privilege of serving as a member of the board of pastors and as youth pastor for many years. Also, I appreciate him, because, with his personal teachings and wise advices, he oriented me to find holiness and to share with others that, as myself, have been called by our glorious Lord JESUS CHRIST to become part of the holly nation.

Thanks to all brothers and sisters in CHRIST from our Central American Evangelical Church "Mies", specially to the youth group; sharing with every one of you I have learned to give my best, because I have received from you all the best of love.

Thanks to Roel Antonio López for his unconditional support towards guiding me through the right way in writing a book oriented to the youth. I appreciate him to involving with dedication and care in reviewing of this material and for guide me in the right way to write a book oriented to the young people.

Thanks to Jennifer Iliana Cárcamo for collaborating writing the reflections for some titles of this book. I also highly appreciate the design on the book's cover.

Thanks to the youth group of the Church Army of GOD from Guatemala City, for their dynamism and passion in the photo session for the cover of this book.

Huge Thanks and all my love to my beloved wife Aura Isabel Tomas, for being by my side holding me up with her love and supporting unconditionally in all the projects and goals that I have undertaking. You are a big blessing from GOD to my life.

All my love and my example to my children Herbert, Pamela, César, Hazell and Pablo; you are heritage from Jehovah and an enormous blessing to my life. You are and have been my reason of inspiring in this life.

All my love and care of a grandfather to my granddaughters Zoe and Emiliana. You are an enormous blessing in my life.

Prefaces

This is the first book in which I am adventuring in the world of literature. I decided to write it, because a special interest in the matter about courtship was born in me while I was the youth pastor at the Evangelical Central American Church "Mies" in Puerto Barrios; for which for several years, there was a need to deal with this subject to find values that young people could apply to their lives to be able to succeed in sentimental relationships. Understanding that, a successful courtship is that accomplishes the objective to be the stage of preparing for marriage.

The need to find wise advices about courtship was reaffirmed in me, because during many years, I could see young Christians of different congregations who were very integrated to the issues of faith and had a lot of cheer to serve the LORD; however as being in a sentimental relationship, without placing values of wisdom, they were led by emotions and neglecting their spiritual lives, they gave up to temptation, and consequently, they got compromised with the sin of fornication. That is, the emotions dragged them to neglect, and being encouraged by culture, they did not notice that Satan has captured cultures of society to filter on it many habits that are very attractive to nature sinful, but they weaken men's spirit making them very vulnerable to temptation. My intention in writing this book is to give elements of wisdom that can help youth to be cautious and to avoid being trapped by those practices and to be able to keep themselves pure and holly during their courtship relationship.

Another problem I saw in courtship relationships of many Christians, and, also ratified in me the need to write this book, is that often, when youth get involved in this kind of relationship, they forget that the main objective of courtship is to prepare them for marriage; therefore, they do not draw towards a wedding ceremony nor to a firm and durable marriage; instead, they simply get involved to satisfy their instinct and to having a good time until with the past of time, they realize if they are or not fit for marriage. My purpose is to give ideas to young people to focus on their courtship in its main objective and to trace the path to follow in order to accomplish that objective.

I do not pretend thru this book to give a magical formula for the success in courtship among Christians. There is no magical formula, and none the less for such a complicated relationship like the courtship. What I intend is to give biblical advices which youth can apply wisely in their lives to not live their courtship according to the ways of the world, but instead, by the vocation that they were called.

GOD bless young persons who may have the opportunity to read this book. May the LORD move their heart to apply in their courtship relationships the values that here are presented to be able to live in holiness and with purpose.

Introduction

The following book has as main objective to give wise advices to young Christians which may help them to live their courtship relationships as it is supposed to be with a son of GOD who is Holy, Holy, Holy; in other words, to live their courtship in holiness and with purpose.

It is convenient to explain the reason why a new Christian courtship book is written. The union of people in couple is a purely cultural affair. This type of relationship varies according to the practices of societies. And as Satan is the god of this world;[1] he has infiltrated perverse practices in the cultures which strengthen the flesh and weaken the spirit of man; especially in those related to courtship. And, how those practices are being infiltrated subtly and gradually, no one is aware of the changes, and when society comes to realize, it is difficult to eradicate them, because they are already rooted in culture and everybody see them as normal rules of behavior. To the societies in this case happens what happens to a frog when someone pretends to cook it: if a person throws a frog into a pot of boiling water, it will jump immediately and flee to save it life. But, if someone puts the same frog in a pot of chilly water that is being heated by the fire, it will be quiet even if the temperature of the water goes up gradually, because it body will adapt to changes in temperature and, without realizing, it will die when boil together with water. This has been happening to society with courtship, because subtle practices that have been added to it, only correspond

---

[1] 2 Corinthians 4:4

to marriage, and now society accepts them as normal. The perversity has been consuming us little by little and, like the frog, we are still as if nothing is happening.

Now, the problem for Christians is that we live in societies that have been adopting bad practices in love relationships; and like the rest of the people, we do not notice that changes, and then, we also find ourselves adopting the current of the world; although, with certain limits, just to make the difference. What is regrettable about this, is that, as the perversity limit of the world rises, so does the level of tolerance of Christian to perversity. For example, there was a time when Christian women wore no pants, because they were taken as provocation to men; but the women of the world wore it, but not very tight, to not fall into indecency. Then, when the women of the world left formal pants to wear tight, the Christian women began to wear formal pants that stopped using non-Christian. And when the women of the world stopped wearing tight-fitting pants to wear lifts tail, Christian women began to wear tight pants, so much so that today it is not uncommon to see young girls attending youth gatherings dressed that way, even with tail lifts. I want to clarify that my example is not to prohibit or condemn the use of trousers among Christian women, but just to support my theory that the limit of permissibility in Christianity has been moving as the limit of perversity of the world moves. Courtship is no exception in this, for it is nowadays common to see Christian couples sharing kisses and caresses in excess, but their thinking is far from marriage; and it is not surprising that some are already having sex believing that it is not sin in the eyes of the Lord.

It is because of all the above written that I ventured to write this my first book. In the seven chapters of this book, I deployed a series of advices (most of them based on the Bible), so that, youth may identify the bad practices of the current courtship and avoid them, so as not to increase the statistics of young Christians who yield to the temptation. My purpose is to provide elements of wisdom which will help young people return to the old paths[2] of engagement and take

---

[2] Jeremiah 6:16

it as the stage of preparation for their marriage, keeping themselves pure and holy to God as they arrive at the wedding ceremony.

This book is aimed at youth who have a serious commitment to holiness. Each word of this work is dedicated to those who courageously have decided to hold the instinct to the wisdom, seeking to do in their courtship everything that is pure, all that is worthy and everything that is of good name, so that, the Lord be glorified by their good testimony. Each word of this book is also directed to young people who are willing to strive to avoid being swept away by the current of worldly thought that perverts the unwary, even if it means having to endure ridicule, rejection and offense from those who, through those attitudes, they want to force them to be just like them. And finally, every word in this book is aimed at young people who love to fulfill their role as salt of the earth and light of the world in a society that needs to be preserved from evil and be enlightened with good works.

May the Lord Jehovah God Almighty, may these words reach the hearts of young readers and help them to change their worldview of the courtship, so that, when they have this kind of relationship, they may do it based on principles that will lead them to stay in holiness and focused on the purpose for which it was created.

Chapter 1

Background of Courtship

Courtship did not always exist in our societies, and when it began, it was not what is practiced today. For a long time in the history, couples did not interact physically under the figure of a stage prior to marriage with the goal of sharing and getting to know each other better. Courtship simply did not exist. To know a little more about this, I will review in history, how the unions of people in couples were given in biblical times, how they were given before the sexual revolution and how they occur now after the sexual revolution.

Relationships of couples in biblical times

In biblical times, it was with the betrothal that the union of people in couples began in Israel. The betrothal was a period of formal and legal commitment that couples contracted prior to marriage. It was like the wedding engagement of our time, but more serious as marriage itself. It was considered unbreakable because it generated a high commitment of future marriage among the bride and groom, so much so that, if any of them wanted to desist from it, it was up to them to do a divorce proceeding. The period of the betrothal lasted about a year.

At the celebration of the beginning of the betrothal, the families of the couple gathered and invited some people who served as witnesses. In the middle of the ceremony, the man gave the woman a garment as a guarantee of wedding engagement by saying the following words: "Serve this garment as a sign of a guarantee that you are reserved for me according to the law of Moses and Israel". After the ceremony, both returned to the homes of their parents, the woman to her daily life and the man to work hard to prepare the goods that would serve as an economic base to the future marriage.

Couples had no physical contact during the betrothal period. The physical interaction between a man and a woman was only permitted until after the wedding celebration. Both, the woman and the man kept distance from each other to avoid any physical interaction. At that time, we could not see romantic scenes between unmarried couples like those we see today.

An important characteristic which stands out from the betrothal is the high commitment of future marriage that generated in the members of the couple. Anyone who got involved in the betrothal did it with the idea of consummating a marriage in the short term. The commitment was so serious that no one engaged in such a relationship unless was ready to marry. The "know us first to see if it works" alternative was an unthinkable option.

Another important characteristic that highlights the betrothal, is the lack of physical interaction of the couple prior to marriage. The man did not think to touch a woman, nor the woman could enter physical contact with the man unless they were married. Chronologically, commitment was before intimacy.

Relationships of couples before the sexual revolution

Until the twentieth century, there was no courtship in much part of Europe and the Americas. People changed their marital status from single to married without going through a stage of transition, preparation or knowledge of each other through sentimental and physical interaction.

At that time, the practice was that, if a man was interested in a young girl; as a first step, he had to go before her parents to request permission to visit her certain days of the week. If they gave their approval, then he began the periodic visits, which consisted of conversations between them, keeping distance to avoid physically contact, and under the strict supervision of her parents. Sometimes during the date, the parents of the young girl sat almost in the middle of the couple controlling the act of both. In those cases, the dialogue was practically between the boy and his future father-in-law. At that time, the physical interaction of the couple began when in the middle of the wedding ceremony the religious minister said to the man "And now you can kiss the bride"; it was until then that the man kissed his girlfriend for the first time. Before that moment he was not even allowed to touch her hands.

The important characteristics that stand out from the relationships of the couple before the sexual revolution remain: the high commitment of future union that generated in the couple and the lack of physical interaction prior to marriage. Which I consider of excellent value for the definition that Christians must handle about courtship.

Relationships of couples after the sexual revolution

The courtship which is practiced in our days arose from a movement that occurred in United States and in Europe called Sexual Revolution. This movement began slightly in the fifties and reached its maximum development between the sixties and eighties; but its effects and consequences are still valid today.

The sexual revolution impacted the courtship practices of society, because it promoted changes in the perception of sexual morality, taking it from the purity it showed towards a severe perversion, even in some sectors of society reached levels of depravation. This movement promoted, since the practice of "Free Love" or "Sex without Marriage", through the practice of "sexual relations without having children", until reaching the "homosexual relationships." Promoting the proposal of "liberal practices", the sexual revolution led us to the generalization of all kinds of sexual relations in courtship, breaking all the moral codes of sexual conduct in force until the fifties. After these changes, the bride and groom no longer necessarily end up marrying, but they do get sexually involved, thereby promoting the proliferation of fornication; a sin from which God commanded to flee, saying that who fornicate against their own body sins.[3]

All the changes proposed by the sexual revolution left negative consequences in the couple relationships: first, it increased in the number of couples that are having sex without being married, because people found very attractive to enjoy the benefits of marriage without assuming its responsibilities; and, if it does not work, the relationship ends without any commitment. Secondly, the marriageable age was delayed, because, as it ceased to be a non-negotiable requirement to have sex, it also ceased became worthwhile to engage in such a serious commitment with many responsibilities. And third, the age to allow to have sex was advanced, because as it was possible to prevent pregnancies using the contraceptive pill, and with the abortion became easy to undo pregnancies, it was appropriate to advance that age, so that, the youth may have different sexual experiences before marriage. As can be seen, these consequences seriously affected the moral codes of conduct in society, in such way that, the perception of seriousness, honor, and purity implied in a couple relationship was disturbed; so as to, what was previously seen as indecent and unacceptable, today looks normal and even as motive to be bullied if it is not done.

Courtship among Christians were also affected by the practices imposed by the sexual revolution. Due to Christians live in societies which have adopted the perverse practices proposed by the sexual revolution movement, they gradually adopted that style of courtship. This is the reason way courtship is a topic which is constantly discussed in youth Christian groups to prevent them from practicing the perversities that are now common in society.

---

[3] 1 Corinthians 6:18

Reflection.

Although difficult to believe, there was a time when courtship did not exist, and all the young people of those times lived very well without it. In those times, the boys did not need a girlfriend, nor did the girls have a boyfriend. They did not think; as many young people today do; that have a love affair before marriage was highly necessary; nor did they think that they could be seriously affected if they did not have a courtship. Because everything is a matter of adapting to an idea of perception of things.

Sadly, the changes which have undergone the relationships of couples have gone from bad to worse, complicating the holiness in which the young Christians want and must live. Changes in the practices of loving union have seriously hit the principles of holiness. However, as everything is a matter of adapting to a way of thinking; then I charge you, as a young Christian, the responsibility not to adapt to the changes that Satan has infiltrated the practices of society, doing the effort to keep you away from this type of thinking and having the complete assurance that, it is possible to conduct yourself as good Christian in your courtship. Because, if the young people who lived until before the fifties could do it, I am sure you also can do, cause it's all a matter of proposing it. You can live your courtship happily keeping you in holiness.

Pray to God asking for wisdom and determination to lead you in the best way possible in your courtship and He will give you, because His ears are attentive to the prayer of His saints.[4]

---

[4] Psalm 34:15

Chapter 2

Definition of Courtship
for Christians

If we talk to a young man about dating, the first thing he will think in a romantic scene where a couple is in some special place, walking hand in hand, watching a sunset and giving them many hugs and kisses. He will think so, because he has been influenced by films, soap operas, musical themes to which he has been exposed since his childhood. And because of having been exposed to those type of information, the worldview he has of the courtship, is that, this is a beautiful stage in which people should spend good times in company of the beloved, wasting intimacy but without responsibilities.

Now, for those are in faith of Jesus, and contrary to what the world dictates; courtship is a loving and formal relationship maintained between a Christian man and woman, with the solid intention of marrying in the short term, in which commitment has more relevance than intimacy and instinct is relegated to wisdom.

Courtship is a loving relationship

For all truly Christians, courtship is a relationship which is based on the biblical principles of true love. For the believer in Jesus Christ, courtship is a relationship that revolves around pure and holy love, characterized by being more action than passion. Christians love is action, because it leads the couple to protect each other so as not to make mistakes, to seek the good of each other, to give honor to each other and to provide the care they need between both to hold in the Lord's will. The love the Christian boyfriends share must be kind, does not behave itself unseemly, seeks not it own, rejoices not in iniquity, hope all things and endure all things.[5]

In the courtship relationships of non-Christians, true love is displaced by "magical passions", which are nothing more than what the apostle Paul calls "disordered passions". The most important thing in the courtship of non-Christians is to please the instinct and feel good. The relationship revolves around a "magical feelings" (seeing stars and hearts, tingling, rapid heartbeat, etc.), which is nourished by love quotes and physical interaction.

Now, in the courtships of Christians, true love controls and displaces the passions to focus on holiness. In Christian couples, the impulses generated by the passions are weakened by actions of holiness which only true love promotes. For example, in a courtship of non-Christians, it is usual for the male; moved by passion; to ask the young woman for the "proof of love (to have sex)" to supposedly be sure that she loves him (this shows that his main interest is to have sex not to love her truly); but, in a courtship of Christian people, the man will not even think of making such that kind of proposal, because he knows that true love seek not its own, does not behave itself unseemly and is kind (putting pressure on his girlfriend to have illicit sex would be very harmful for her), in addition, the security of their relationship would not rest in a sinful action, but in attitudes of justice.

Passion should not be the foundation of courtship between Christians, just the true love, which is pure and holy.

---

[5] Corinthians 13:4-7

Courtship is a formal relationship

For the young saved by Jesus Christ, courtship is a relationship which is characterized by being formal. A loving relationship between Christians is not a child's play, on the contrary, it is a serious matter that does not allow immature children to play to the little boyfriends; because, as it is a relation regarding marriage, it must be perceived as serious and formal.

Christians bride and groom are demanded to fulfill all the formalities necessary to ensure the stability and seriousness of their courtship relationship. These formalities begin first, to inform the parents of both about their intentions and request their approval before initiate the relationship. Secondly, inform the rest of families of both is also necessary, because when the marriage be consummated, the couples become part of the families respectively. Third, they should inform their spiritual leaders of their intentions, because shepherds are who can give the best reference about the level spiritually of their sheep, and their feedback should be considered very important for the consummation of the relationship. And fourthly, the bride and groom must inform the whole congregation once the courtship has been formalized, so that, is necessary the brothers in faith know about the new relationship.

Anything that shows seriousness, respect, and good name for the courtship should be added to the courtship of Christians. It is very important to do everything in order, with clarity and transparency to give a good testimony of formality to the relationship.

Courtship is a relationship between a man and a woman

For those are in faith of Jesus, courtship is a loving relationship between a man and a woman. A Christian engagement can only occur between people of opposite sex, because from the beginning, God created the male and the woman to be complementary to each other.[6] A man is not complementary to another man nor a woman

---

[6] Genesis 1:27

to another woman. Ignoring this, is to go against the nature that God gives in man and woman. Courtship among Christians is a relationship that is based on the natural design of God, therefore, it must be between male and female.

Any loving relationship between people of the same sex is abominable the Lord.[7] God clearly forbids a man to have sex with another man, because it is an unbearable sin in His presence. But Satan has deceived society into believing that "love" is the most important thing in a relationship, regardless of whether they are of the same sex. However, the Bible declares that the Lord detests homosexual relationships, so much so, that He sentences those who practice it not to enter the Kingdom of Heaven.[8] So, every love relationship must be between a man and a woman so that God does not disqualify it.

Homosexual unions violate the preservation of the human on this planet. Common sense indicates that God created both, male and female, to mate and procreate children; that guarantees the preservation of the human species on this earth. Now imagine that all men marry men, and all women marry women; it would happen that, over a period, humanity would end. In conclusion, in the more homosexual relationships exists, the more danger is in the preservation of the human on earth.

Recall then that; as courtship is the preparation for marriage, and when God instituted marriage it was between a man and a woman; all Christian courtship must only occur between people of the opposite sex, otherwise is abomination to God.

Courtship is a relationship between Christian people

For God's children, Christian courtship is a loving relationship between the children of God. It is a relationship between two people who have a common faith practice grounded in Jesus Christ as their Lord and Savior.

---

[7] Leviticus 18:22
[8] 1 Corinthians 6:9-10

Christians should not unite in loving relationships with unbelievers. The Lord commanded in His Word not to unite in unequal yoke with unbelievers, because light and darkness have no fellowship with each other and neither does Christ with Satan.[9] This means that a Christian should not join in courtship with a non-Christian; because, spiritually speaking, they do not have things in common, Christian people are interested in pleasing God with theirs acts, but the unbelievers are interested in pleasing themselves. For this reason, every believer must be obedient to the Word of God and not be sentimentally involved in an unequal yoke with an unbeliever.

The Christian youth of today do not give due importance to obeying the commandment not to unite in loving relationship with unbelievers. Perhaps because of the lack of awareness of what it means to be a Christian, young people take this mandate very briefly, and they try to justify in one and thousand ways their decision to become romantically involved with someone who is not of their same faith. But such justifications will not help them mitigate the tough times that they will experience as consequence of their disobedience. Because God cannot be mocked, for whatsoever a man soweth, that shall he also reap.[10]

This topic will be discussed in more detail in the title " Look for a loving partner within Christians" in Chapter 5.

Courtship is a relationship that aims to prepare the couple for marriage

For believers, courtship is primarily intended to prepare the couple for marriage. Just as in the betrothal, Christians who engage in a dating relationship must assume the firm intention of getting married in the short or at the latest in the medium term. The seriousness of courtship gives no chance to be playing without focusing on fulfilling their main purpose. That is why Christians

---

[9] 2 Corinthians 6:14
[10] Galatians 6:7

should plan to have their courtship concluded at the wedding ceremony, so that, from then on, they can start a successful marriage.

A Christian should not engage in a loving relationship if he does not intend to marry. In the world people have their dating relationship only to pass the time, in most cases. But for Christians, dating must create an elevated level of commitment to future marriage.

From the beginning of the relationship, Christian bride and groom must commit to marriage. They should agree that, only for some reason which is completely beyond the control of both, they may accept that the relationship ends without marriage.

Courtship is a relationship in which commitment has more relevance than intimacy

For those are in faith of Jesus Christ, courtship is a relationship in which, the commitment has more relevance than intimacy. As in the biblical model of betrothal, Christian bridegrooms must make compromises before moving on to caresses, hugs and kisses. They must talk with their parents, set an approximate date of wedding celebration and all formal commitments that the relationship requires before moving on to cautious intimacy.

In most of today's courtships, much intimacy is shared but little commitment is acquired. The widespread practice that inherited the sexual revolution to the courtship is that, people should have all kinds of intimacy experiences first, and after, the commitments should have acquired, if there is little space to think about them. That is why if you see a couple very sweetheart and then you ask them if they plan to marry, they will respond you that they are still not crazy. They love intimacy, but they shy away from commitment.

Christians should eliminate from their courtship the bad practice of giving more importance to the affective exchange than the commitments that the relationship entails. In Christian courtship, physical interactions must take less priority than the commitments of the relationship. Doing this will return the spirit of commitment with the courtship began and avoid failures in their love relationships.

Courtship is a relationship in which the instinct is dominated by wisdom

In courtship among Christians, instinct is dominated by wisdom. Wisdom controls the instinctive reaction of "going beyond" in intimacy when bodies come into contact through hugs, caresses and kisses. That instinctive reaction is natural in the behavior of the human being, because God created us to be sexually attractive between man and woman. But it must also be natural for Christians couples to be wise to control the instinct, because, through the Holy Spirit, God gave the power of self-control in people who believe in Jesus Christ.[11]

People who lived before the 1950s understood very well the nature of the human in reaction to the stimulus of the opposite sex. And to avoid stumbling, the boyfriends were not allowed physical contact. But since society has allowed all kinds of physical interaction between the bride and groom, the risk of not controlling those reactions is extremely high; so, it is good to avoid constant friction, prolonged appointments, secluded places, excessive caresses and everything else that encourages sexual intercourse.

The wise man fears and departs from evil says the word of the Lord.[12] As wise young Christians, bride and groom should turn away from all temptation to master the instinct with wisdom during their dating relationship. This is the only way to maintain a relationship as it suits saints.

Reflection.

The first thing about you, as a Christian, must be convinced is that you live in this world but you are not part of it.[13] Your citizenship is not from this earth, but from the Celestial Kingdom.[14] That is why the Lord

---

[11] Galatians 5:22-23
[12] Proverbs 14:16
[13] John 17:16
[14] Philippians 3:20

demands you to live as a worthy representative of the Holly Kingdom here on earth in all areas of your life.

The advises of Word of God for you in order to live as a worthy representative of the Heavenly Kingdom here on earth, are to not adopt the practices of the world in your life, but to transform yourself through the renewing of your mind.[15] That, among other things, means you must to ensure that, do not contaminate your mind with the unpleasant habits practiced in the world today by making you believe they are normal. This I express, because people easily adapt to everything that is in their social environment, without discerning sometimes if it is good or not to please God. This is the case of courtship that are practiced today in many societies. For example, you might perceive normal that young people have a loving affair only because they liked each other regardless of whether or not they are ready for marriage; because after all, what matters according to your mind, is that, if there is love between them it is enough. I also know that, if you have already liked somebody, it is certain that you have already dreamed awake with beloved, with romantic scenes in a beach where both walk together holding hands, seeing a full moon that adorns the scenery of your dreams. You have that kind of dream, because it's what you've seen in movies or among your fellow students or among your neighbors, etc. But if I ask you if, along with that dream you would like to place another scene in which you are working hard to feed your wife with three or four children, you will surely tell me that you do not want it, because what you have learned in your social environment is that you should enjoy the benefits of courtship without adopting the commitments it entails.

The courtship practices that the world offers you today will be more detrimental than beneficial to your spiritual life if you are not wise. In the world, people do what the devil says, because he is the god of this age.[16] And his interest is the all people in this world live against the principles that the Lord has established. Unfortunately, he has almost succeeded in his intentions, because the perverse practices he introduced in courtship are the main reason why more than thirteen million children are born every year in the world, whose mothers are young women between the ages of

---

[15] Romans 12:2

[16] 2ª Corinthians 4:4

ten and nineteen,[17] they are also the causes why the world has more than forty million abortions on average each year.[18] To avoid being part of those statistics, I advise you to practice what the Word of the Lord exhorts you to do: Do not adopt the practices of courtship that the world proposes, however amusing and attractive they may seem to you; but do your best effort to practice a courtship which is worthy of people washed by the Blood of the Holy Lamb.

To practice a courtship worthy of Christians, you should restrict in your relationship the permissive limits that allow to satisfy the carnal pleasures. Take out of your mind the idea of "try to see if it works" because that will lead you to have several lovers and may hurt you. Take out of your mind the idea of overcoming yourself in physical contact with your bridegrooms, because that can lead you to sin. And finally, take out of your mind the idea of enjoying sex in your courtship, because it is sin and distorts what a courtship is between Christians.

Although the world has distorted the courtship, (taking away the pure and the special and using it to satisfy the carnal pleasures) you, as a citizen of the Celestial Kingdom here on earth, should not fall into that trap, because you deserve to live in the higher level of life that God expects of His redeemed saints. Seek with a renewed mind according to the mind of Christ to honor the Name of the Lord by living a relationship of courtship according to true love, applying wisdom, temperance and patience. If you do this, I assure you with all my heart that you will be happy.

---

[17] Wikipedia - Pregnancy in adolescents
[18] GloboMeter - Number of abortions in the world.

Chapter 3

Appropriate age for Christians to begin with courtship relationship

Establishing an appropriate age to initiate a courtship relationship generates controversy in many societies. Because, on one side are those who maintain the criteria that the age is not important if there is love between the couple; and on the other side are those who believe that it is necessary to reach an age of mental and emotional maturity, because courtship must conclude in a marriage. It is very difficult for society to agree on this issue, however, I believe that Christians should have defined an average minimum age in which young people may start with a courtship relationship, so that parents have a reference to authorize that kind of relationships of their children and also to help the same youth not to engage in a premature courtship.

To suggest an approximate minimum age which serve as a reference for Christians to begin a courtship relationship, I will first discuss the factors which, in my opinion, are involved in it.

Development of the human body

The development of the human body is the main factor to define the average age at which Christians may begin a courtship relationship. The development of the body awakens the attraction of human to another of the opposite sex, due to physical, mental and emotional changes that lead them from childhood to adults capable of sexual reproduction. So, the child whose main hobby was the game of cars or little guns, once these changes began, he invests considerable part of his time to admire the beauty of the woman, wanting to approach to caress her and share all his love with her. And at the same time, the girl, whose main hobby was the game with dolls, suddenly changes her priority and invests considerable part of her time in personal care to look more beautiful and attractive to the male, because now she wants to be by his side to feel protected and loved. The development of the human body is the trigger of the mutual attraction between the male and the female. This is the main factor that influences the determination of the average age at which Christians should have their first courtship relationship.

Normally, according to professionals in matter, the development of the body occurs between the ages of ten and eleven in women, and between the ages of thirteen and fourteen in males. At those ages, the adolescents begin to experience the sensation that somebody likes them, and, they begin to have their first fantasies of courtship, because it awakes in them the instinct which the Lord gives of being complementary to each other.[19] When teenagers reach those ages, they become vulnerable to the desire to have a loving relationship and feel that they have the right to engage in a courtship to satisfy their feelings of attraction. However, experiencing that feelings does not mean they are already prepared for marriage, and if they are not ready for marriage, they are not ready for courtship either.

If the appropriate age for begin a courtship relationship depends only on this factor, I would say that Christians are able to start that kind of relationship when they feel attracted to the opposite sex.

---

[19] Genesis 2:20-24

However, since the appropriate age not only depends on this factor, I will analyze the second to establish the average age suggested.

Mental and emotional maturity

Mental and emotional maturity is also another crucial factor required for Christians to initiate a courtship relationship; because, although on the one hand, the hormones impel the youth to desire to have a loving affair at an early age, it is sure that at that age, they have not yet matured enough to begin with that kind of relationship.

Mental and emotional maturity, according to experts in the matter, is described as the culminating point of the process of growth and development of the human being body; which consists in the integration and consolidation of various qualities of the whole person, from the physical, the psychological and the spiritual. That is, the person has achieved a harmony and proportion between the way of living and human nature.

According to the experts in the matter, a person reaches the mental and emotional maturity between the twenty and the twenty-one years in average. At that age is when the qualities of the whole person have been consolidated, forming a human being able to take responsibly in decisions that concern his life using the free will that God gave him.

Christians must wait to have mental and emotional maturity to engage in a loving relationship, because doing so before, it can be more harmful than beneficial, so immature attitudes can cause emotional injuries that affect one or both in the long term.

Economic ability to support a home

The ability to sustain a home economically is another important requirement for Christians to enter a courtship relationship. The couple, or at least the male, should be economically active to engage in a relationship, whose main purpose is to form a family. An economically active person is one who has a job or who is fit to have one. So, if the believers want to get involved in a romantic relationship, they should have a job or at least they should be looking for one.

The average age at which a person acquires the ability to sustain a home financially may vary depending on the practices of the society. In rural societies, it is common for persons to become economically active between the ages of twelve and fifteen, because to get a job and earn to support their life economically, they only need the empirical knowledge of a job. This knowledge acquires them from their parents, who through the practical teaching transmit the knowledge to them to carry out in a task and thus to be able to maintain a family. However, in urban societies the minimum age to be an economically active person increases as the knowledge is diversified. For example, until the middle of the last century persons did not require much academic preparation to perform a professional job, having attended elementary school was enough to qualify for an excellent job and earn to support their life economically. If we translate this to age, a person was prepared between the ages of twelve and seventeen years. However, as of the end of the 20th century, the age to be economically active increased, because, as knowledge diversified, there was a need for specialization in each area and therefore high school, college and university studies became necessary to compete in the working market. Therefore, the minimum age moved to twenty-three and so far, years on average. In short, the age to be prepared to support a family economically depends on the practices of the society in which people live.

Regardless of the age at which people acquire the ability to sustain a household financially, the important thing is to have that ability to engage in a courtship relationship. Because if the main purpose of courtship is to marry and to form a family, they must have the capacity to generate the essential income to cover all the expenses to satisfy the basic needs of that family.

Defining the appropriate age

After reviewing the development of the human being body, mental and emotional maturity, and the ability to economically support a home, I define that, the approximate age to initiate a courtship relationship is the age at which a person feels attraction by the opposite sex, is prepared physically, mentally and emotionally, and has the economic capacity to support a family. No Christians should have a courtship relationship if they do not meet these three requirements.

What to do while reach the appropriate age to have courtship relationship

Be patient

Young Christians should strive to be patient to wait until they are physically, mentally, emotionally, and financially ready for a courtship relationship. Surely many young people will think that it is impossible to fulfill the three requirements that I propose, because the gap between the time the body opens its eyes to love and the time in which those requirements can be met is at least ten years. That means they must have the enough patience to wait for those ten long years, fighting against the demands of hormones, against the erotic bombardment of the media, against the pressure of friends and against the feeling of "If everyone does it, why cannot I do it?". To win the battle, young people should remember that the fruit of the Holy Spirit produces in the Christian an attribute called "self-control",[20] which will help them to have control over their emotions and their impulses. They should only use that attribute to have patience and wait until have the appropriate age to start a dating relationship.

Have determination to live in purity

Self-determination to remain pure and holy in presence of the Lord should also be a source of motivation for young Christians to not engage prematurely in a courtship relationship. Just as Daniel,

---

[20] Galatians 5:22-23

Ananias, Misael, and Azariah, decided to keep themselves pure in presence of the Lord by rejecting the food of King Nebuchadnezzar,[21] so also young Christians should keep themselves pure away from the mundane practices of engaging in a premature courtship; the greatest risk of having that kind of relationship is to yield to the temptation and therefore lose purity.

Imitate those who lived before the sexual revolution

If unbelieving youth who lived until before the fifties could withstand internal and external pressures and abstained from seeking a couple relationship when they were not prepared, the young Christians of today, who have the Holy Spirit empowering them with self-control, will be able to endure and wait patiently for be prepared to start their courtship relationship. Imitating the youth who lived before the sexual revolution in patience and control over feelings will help young Christians of this generation to wait the time to be the appropriate age to begin with a courtship relationship.

Reflection.

Everything has its opportune moment in the life and there is a specific time for everything that is done in this earth.[22] Everything that is done in the life of human being has a propitious moment to be carried out with success. Anticipating to that moment, can seriously affect the conclusion of what is done, so much so, that may negatively mark the life of a person. For example, if you would give a crowded bus to a seven-year-old boy to be the driver, is highly probable to occur a major accident which damages the same child and all bus passengers; that would happen because it is not the perfect time in the life of this child to drive a collective vehicle. But when that child grows up and comes of age and receives training for the safe and effective driving of the bus, then it will be the right time to do so, then the risk of accident will have diminished, since he will be able to be driver.

---

[21] Daniel 1:8
[22] Ecclesiastes 3:1

Courtship has its opportune time to be successful in people's lives. There is an appropriate time in your life to start with a loving relationship. That moment you will identify it, because it will be when you be prepared physically, mentally, emotionally and economically. If you engage in a love relationship without being prepared; just like the bus boy driver sample; it is very likely that you will crash in your future and affect you seriously as well as many people who are around, you. Now, if you have the patience to wait for that moment, you will have less risk of failure, because by then, you will have the ability to handle this kind of relationship efficiently, controlling each of its phases.

A virtue that you must try to exploit to wait for the opportune moment to initiate your courtship, is the patience. The Spirit of Christ who dwells in you, will enable you; as part of His fruit in you; to develop the patience you need to expect without delay the opportune moment to start your courtship. Just as a pregnant woman waits patiently for nine months for her child to form in her womb until the perfect time for the birth of a healthy and complete child arrives, so you must also have the patience to wait for your body, you mind, your emotions and your economic capacity will mature until you be ready to handle a courtship relationship.

Try to be patient in waiting for the right moment to have a courtship relationship, and while that moment arrives, strive to prepare the best you can, so that, when your turn comes, you may start your relationship in the best way possible. For just as a worm waits patiently for its metamorphosis which will make it a beautiful butterfly, so also the patient waiting for the opportune moment will lead you to have a successful courtship.

Chapter 4

Christians and Premature Courtship

Premature courtship

Premature courtship is the pretense of loving before time. It is a love relationship which occurs when one of the couple is not physically, mentally, emotionally and economically prepared. In other words, it is having a boyfriend or girlfriend when they are not yet ready to marry.

Consequences of premature courtship

The consequences that may affect those who involved in a premature courtship are many; however, below I describe two of them.

Dishonor parents for unauthorized courtship

Engaging in premature courtship leads youth into secret relationships, which dishonors parents. Due to parents generally do not authorize their children to have a sentimental partner at an early age, they tend to rebel in disobedience and have hidden dates. Consequently, they are forced to arrange their dates in secluded or dark places. Now, What honor is there for a parent who receives comments that his son or daughter was in a hidden place with somebody? The answer is none, because what a father longs for, is that his children do everything to feel honored.

On the other hand, rebelling against parents having unauthorized courtships is also cataloged as an act of injustice. Having hidden courtship is unfair because missing the approval of people who have been taking care of children from childhood to youth, only to please a stranger is very ungrateful. Parents are wearing down to provide daily sustenance, clothing, education, and everything the children need to grow. Not to give value to that effort, by indulging in a courtship without their authorization, is an act of injustice, because it is doing less and turning away from the earthly person who deserves all consideration, all respect and all honor from those were begotten, nourished and raised by them. Christians should not act with injustice, because it is a sin that seriously damages interpersonal relationships, including one very important as is parents with their children.

To maintain living in justice, young Christians should not engage in a premature courtship, and even less without the consent of their parents; especially because they must show their love for their parents giving them the honor, so that God may repay them with long days of life here on earth.[23]

To yield to the temptation of illicit sex

The most serious consequence of premature courtship is to yield to the temptation of illicit sex. As this type of courtship is doomed to be very extensive, the couple accumulate many physical experiences for a long time, which instinctively makes their bodies to ask to go beyond the innocent kisses to pass on sexual experiences more compromising.

Young Christian must avoid illicit sex by turning away from all fornication and uncleanness that is not suited to the saints.[24] For this, they must be wise and flee from evil by turning away from all that

---

[23] Exodus 20:12
[24] Ephesians 5:3

can make them give in to the temptation to fornicate. And as early courtship paves the way for access to that sin, then it is the first thing that every good Christian must flee.

The consequence of illicit sex brings with its other repercussions to the young people who practice them, and I outline some of them.

1. **It affects the believer's relationship with their Lord.**

Any sin affects the relationship between Christian and God, especially the fornication, because it attacks the temple of God, which is the body of the believer.[25] Fornication causes the believers to lose good fellowship with their Lord. Their devotional life is affected, because they lose interest in prayer, in reading the Word and in regularly attending the congregation.

Illicit sex will also cause the Christians to temporarily lose peace that surpasses all understanding. The Holy Spirit will rebuke them of sin and will not leave them alone until they confess, ask for forgiveness, and turn away from that sin.

Fornication is detrimental to the believer's relationship with God and therefore it is necessary for the Christian to be wise and make every effort not to engage in a premature engagement and thus avoid yielding to the temptation of that sin.

2. **Woman is dishonored to lose her virginity.**

Contrary to what the world wants to appear, every woman is dishonored when loses her virginity without being married. For God, the virginity of the woman has a very high value, so much that, He instructed to His priests to marry solely

---

[25] 1 Corinthians 6:18

and exclusively with virgin women.[26] The Lord put the seal of virginity on the woman so that on the first wedding night the covenant of marriage be sealed with blood, because in all the covenants that He has established, there must be blood to be valid. To lose the virginity without being married is a disgrace for every woman, because there is no serious pact to confirm before God at bedtime with a man in those conditions.

When a woman loses her virginity not being married, is exposed to continue sinning with one and with another man. After having her first sexual experience, it is very difficult for a considerable number of young women to stop practicing sex, thereby increasing the likelihood of having sex with each boyfriend they have. This affects woman reputation, because her honor, the honor of her future husband and the honor of her future children rests in her modesty.

Men must also value the woman's virginity in order not to dishonor her. A woman does not lose her virginity alone, she needs a male to consummate the fact. The man who consumes that fact, is responsible before God of that woman's virginity and they have to account for it.[27] Males should then take care not to walk hummingbirds by damaging young girls by making them lose their virginity only for the pleasure of having them for a while in bed; because, in my opinion, that makes them co-responsible before the Lord, because they impelled them to that way.

Satan has deceived society into believing that woman's virginity has no value. In these last decades, the devil has popularized the idea that a young girl can give her virginity to a man, if he makes her spend a "magic" moment for being

---

[26] Leviticus 21:13-15
[27] Deuteronomy 22:28-29

the first time, even if they are not married; and she will feel no remorse after doing so. What the devil has concealed is the frustration young girls feel when they lose their virginity in a passing relationship; this frustration occurs because the most natural thing is that a woman feels dirty and used to sleep with a male for the first time without being married, knowing that nothing guarantees that this man will honor her after he has already got the most precious from her. In order not to fall into the devil's trickery, the young women should ignore all the advice, recommendations and challenges that lead them to go to bed with a man without being married.

To maintain the privilege of becoming virgins to marriage, it is advisable young women not to engage in sentimental relationships at an early age, thereby not exposing themselves to the risk of yielding to the temptation of illicit sex and thereby losing their virginity.

3. **An unwanted pregnancy.**

An unwanted pregnancy is also a latent possibility because of illicit sex. The natural thing to happen when a man and a woman have sex is pregnancy, regardless of whether the couple wants it or not, or whether they are prepared to support a child or not; because God created the human being to reproduce through such relationships, whether lawful or not. Therefore, the risk of unwanted pregnancy is high when young people give in to the temptation to have sex without being married.

An unwanted pregnancy can have serious repercussions for the couple: First, being a single mother, this occurs when the male refuses to accept the responsibility of being a father and leaves the young woman with all responsibilities of giving birth and growing the son. Second, a forced marriage, in which case the young are forced to accept the consequences of their acts venturing into a premature marriage. And thirdly, abortion, in which case the young people see as the only option to exit of their error "undoing" the pregnancy, murdering their helpless son. The repercussions of an unwanted pregnancy will strongly affect the life of both the male and the female.

Unwanted pregnancies have affected the dreams of many young people. The plans of several boys have been truncated because of a pregnancy they did not expect. For example, many young men who dreamed to be university professionals ended up working as maintenance laborers because they had to take responsibility for the maintenance of their wife and son, for that forced them to drop out of college and the dream of being professionals. An unwanted pregnancy will drastically affect the plans of young people who decide to get sexually involved when they are not married.

Young people who do not engage in premature dating will not risk unwanted pregnancy because they will not be exposed to the temptation of illicit sex. I recommend to young people to keep living in wisdom and avoid such relationships.

Premature courtship is not for Christian people

No Christian should engage in premature courtship relationship. We have already said that courtship is not child's play, on the contrary, it is a relationship that requires special preparation of those involved. Because of this, in Christian environments, it should not be usual to see couples of teenage having dating, neither parents and spiritual leaders consenting to such kind of relationships.

Even with parental approval, it is not desirable for young Christians to engage in premature courtship. There are parents who authorize their children to have a sentimental partner when they are not in the proper age. They justify it by saying (so defeatistly) that they authorize it to prevent their children from having a clandestine courtship. However, what those parents forget, is that they should educate their children to be obedient in presence or absence of them to go well in their life and be blessed by the Lord. They also forget that; a premature engagement entails the same risks with or without their authorization. Parents who authorize their children to have courtship at an early age are practically pushing them to the roulette of failure. That is why parental consent should not be enough reason for young Christians to engage in a premature dating relationship, because the effect of such authorization is likely to be detrimental to them.

Although they feel a strong attraction towards a person, young Christians must avoid being romantically involved with that person when they are not yet at the proper age. Since, just as well sin does not suit holiness, the premature courtship does not suit to Christians.

Reflection.

The wise Christian fears and departs from evil so that their lives be not negatively marked.[28] Just as Joseph fled wisely from Potiphar's wife when he sexually harassed him, so the wise Christians must flee from premature courtship, so that, their lives be not affected by the adverse consequences that it can generate. It is wise for them to turn away from all evil to avoid bad experiences.

A premature engagement will probably mark your life in a negative way. Surely your longing is that your courtship be a very special relationship and that ends in a happy marriage; not only because the wedding ceremony be beautiful, but also because all conjugal life is founded on good principles so that it lasts until death separates them. But if you venture into a dating relationship before being prepared physically, mentally, emotionally and financially, it is very likely that your pretensions of happiness will not be fulfilled, because you will surely experience tricky situations, which will

---

[28] Proverbs 14:16

leave you with bad experiences and sad memories. Because to venture into a premature courtship, is like trying to cross a bridge that is half-built in a car that travels at high speed; the chances are that you will have unfavorable consequences, due to the risk situations that usually occur. It is not good for you to start a courtship if you are not yet at the right age. If you do, chances are that your life will be affected.

Many young girls who had dreamed of having a husband who was a man of good, being responsible, good Christian, who became a good father and all the innumerable good virtues possible, ended up related to a man who not even in shadows is what they had dreamed, all for not having the patience to wait for the opportune moment. In the same way, some young men who had also dreamed of having a virtuous woman as a couple, ended up relating to women of bad life, whose moral practices are very distant from a virtuous woman, also for not having the patience to wait for the appropriate moment.

Just as there is no merit in forgiving someone who has not offended you, there is also no merit in expecting something that you do not long for. If you long for a good dating relationship and mark your life positively, you must be patient and wait until you are fully prepared. It is not crazy to wait, nor it is crazy to be patient; what it costs, COST! not only because our body itself screams to have a sentimental couple, but also because the world oversees putting everything at our disposal to make it easy the mistake of anticipating having a partner when still we are not prepared.

God is not mistaken, when He tells you not to trust in your own prudence,[29] nor when He tells you that on all things kept, guard your heart.[30] It is good for you, then, not to be carried away by your feelings, nor by your emotions, but be prudent and patient in waiting. I understand, that waiting is not pleasant, being patient is not easy and being obedient most of the time turns out to be even more difficult and less pleasant, especially when the hormones impel you to look for a partner, and with the aggravating of living in the middle of a society that push you everywhere, so that, you give in and decide to get involved in a love relationship prematurely. But I also understand that we have a God who has placed

---

[29] Proverbs 3:5
[30] Proverbs 4:23

in us a Spirit of power, love and self-control,[31] *who will strengthen you to withstand internal and external pressures and thus act in patience. Once again, I tell you that, it will not be easy, but without fear of being wrong, I also tell you that, it will be worth doing your best effort and waiting. The Holy Spirit who dwells in you will sustain you with His power to strengthen you in the temperance and patience you need to withstand any pressure that causes you to have a premature engagement.*

Be wise and run away from a premature courtship relationship so that you live fully every stage of your life and not suffer bad experiences which can leave you bad memories or frustrations for not having reached your dreams.

---

[31] 2 Timothy 1:7

Chapter 5

Actions Christians execute to choose their loving partner wisely

Young Christians usually choose their loving partner wisely. To choose a couple carries a lot of seriousness and responsibilities, because it is choosing, nothing more and nothing less than, the person with whom will live for the rest of life. That is enough reason why the youth must act in a sober, intelligent and prudent manner in that election. And to help them, I present a series of actions which they may apply in order to do this task successfully.

To get out the circle of feelings

To choose the couple wisely, I suggest youth to leave the circle of feelings and enter the circle of intelligence. Youth will choose better if they put aside the emotions that generate the feelings and replace them with the objectivity generated by the intelligence. Leaving the circle of feelings will make youth to choose wisely because they will have objectively evaluated all the favorable and unfavorable aspects of the person to choose.

Choosing under the influence of feelings will make youth to be guided more by emotion than by conviction. This will lead them to make a very superficial evaluation of the person to choose, because their criteria will be: "I like him or her", "is handsome or pretty", "is the most popular of the school or congregation", "makes me feel happy "," we make a good couple ", etc. Many youths who have chosen this way have ended up frustrated because they neglected to evaluate the kind of person the guy or girl was, and they had a pleasant surprise when they realized that beloved was not what they expected. Choosing under the influence of feelings can bring consequences not very favorable to young Christians.

Now, choosing under the influence of intelligence will make youth to choose more reasoning than with the heart. Their criteria for choosing will be: "is Christian", "has spiritual maturity", "has good principles", "has good education", "gets along with his family", "is responsible", etc. This type of evaluation helps to define whether to join the person, visualizing the relation to the future. For example, if the chosen person has good principles, will surely be a good spouse; if is responsible, surely will fulfill all the commitments of the future home; if get along well with his current family, will certainly strive to keep his future family together, because that will be for excellent value to him. In conclusion, if youth choose their partner intelligently they will have a successful courtship and therefore a stable marriage.

One practice that I advise youth to execute in order to choose their loving partner with intelligence, is to think as if they are choosing a couple for a loved one and want to choose the right person for him or her. This will help them to completely get out of the circle of feelings and look for a person who, for the future, be good spouse or good father or good mother, and who loves God above all things, and all the good virtues which be need it to have a good marriage. My endorsement for this advice is that, in biblical times, those who chose the couple for sons and daughters were the parents and they did not even ask them if they liked the other person or not, they just had to accept the chosen one, because it was the will of their parents. This type of choice had its advantages, because being outside the influence of feelings, the parents chose intelligently, they evaluated the person very well, analyzing their values as a priority before their physical attributes. As a result, marriages were very stable and prosperous; proof of this is that there were not as many divorces as there are in our days. If youth take this advice, they will leave in background the physical attraction and all those superficialities by which they choose their loving partners today and will focus on analyzing whether it is convenient for them to join a person, evaluating their values.

It is necessary that youth leave the circle of feelings to make an intelligent choice of their loving partner, because the wise Christians choose their loving partner with the mind and not with the heart.

Hold in high regard the advice of the parents

To choose wisely the loving partner, the youth should have in high esteem the advice of their parents. The perspective that parents have about life is very different than the youth have, since the experience they have makes them more objective in the evaluation of the person to whom they will give their son or daughter to live the rest of their days. They will assess aspects such as education, the principles of life, the kind of family they come from, the church in which they congregate, the level of commitment to the Lord's work, and other important aspects that youth do not usually take into consideration when choosing. It is very important that youth take advantage of the valuable advice of their parents to add wisdom to the election and thus minimize the risks of failure in their courtship relationship.

The willingness of children to obey their parents' advice is also important to do an excellent choice. It is not enough just to listen to the advice of the parents, but also to obey them and put them in practice. That is, the advice of parents should be taken as mandatory, because obeying them will always benefit the sons and daughters, since parents usually never want evil for them, but always seek good. So, I suggest youth to pay close attention to their parents' recommendations about the person to choose and take them as a mandate to obey, because behind a good advice is always a good intention of the one who gives and a benefit for who receives it.

I want to motivate youth to be obedient to the recommendations of their parents when choosing their loving partner, because that will help them to clarify the criteria, they have about the person to choose and therefore make a wise choice. The obedience of the children to the parents brings good consequences to those who practice it, because God blesses them.

Look for a loving partner within Christians

To make a wise choice, young Christians should seek a mate within the same Christian people. Christians have been constituted as a holy nation, called to glorify the name of God, living in holiness and removed from all contamination of the world around them.[32] Aware of the privilege of belonging to this holy nation, young Christians must make the decision not to become contaminated by joining in loving relationships with people who are not Christians.[33] Every Christian has the obligation not to unite in unequal yoke with unbelievers in order not to suffer later consequences.[34]

The Christians who seek a mate outside the Christian people demonstrate among other things that they:

1. **Have not realized the privilege of belonging to a holy nation.**

   The Christians who engage with unconverted one demonstrate that they have not realized the privilege of belonging to the people that the Lord bought at the price of Blood to remove them from darkness, to be part of the holy nation and live on a higher level of life, without

---

[32] 1 Peter 2:9
[33] Genesis 24:3-4
[34] 2 Corinthians 6:14

contamination with sin.[35] Neither have they realized that, the Christians have been rescued from a vain way of life, which had them condemned to the fire of hell, so that, in gratitude for their rescue, they live dedicated to God in all aspects of their life, not giving place their sainthood at risk.

Christians who relate sentimentally to unbelievers have not realized the privilege of behaving like a Christian and being called children of God, nor have they valued the price God paid for their liberation, much less have they sized the meaning of word holiness.

2. **Have not understood that the holy and the profane should not be mixed.** [36]

The Christians who engage sentimentally with unconverted people demonstrate that, they have not understood that just as Christ has no relation to Satan[37] and as light has no fellowship with darkness; so, the Christian should not have loving communion with an unconverted person. They also show that they have not understood that, just as water and oil cannot be mixed, so the holiness and the profane either, because at the presence of God it is like wanting to unite holiness with sin.

For the Lord, the mixture of the holiness and the profane is an abomination. In the biblical history of Israel, we can see that on several times, the Lord severely rebuked them for mixing the holy and the profane. It is to be expected then the rebuke from God to those who being their holy children mingle with unbelievers.

---

[35] 1 Peter 2:9
[36] Ezekiel 44:23
[37] 2 Corinthians 6:16

The Christians who engage sentimentally with the non-Christians, show that they have not understood the high meaning of God's holiness as reducing it by mixing it with the profane.

3. **Give more importance to their will than to God.**

The Christians who engage in a loving relationship with a worldly person demonstrate that is more important for them to please their desires than to please the commands of the Lord. All Christians should have as a priority to please God rather than men, including them self,[38] doing the contrary is idolatry.

They also demonstrate that they have not learned to deny them self, to take up their cross and follow Christ.[39] The Christians must refuse to comply with the demands of the sinful nature, withstanding the internal pressures which this generates, and thus overcome the desires of the flesh to live according to the will of God. Engaging with unbelievers only demonstrates that the person's ego is much stronger than the conviction of yielding to the will of God.

And lastly, it demonstrates that they have not learned to wane for Christ to grow in them.[40] They have not learned that the Christians should wreck their personal interests and let the interests of Christ take priority in them, nor have they learned that they must crucify the natural egocentrism which leads them to concentrate on their personal interests so that Christ lives in them taking control of their interests and their decisions.[41]

---

[38] Acts 4:19
[39] Lucas 9:23
[40] John 3:30
[41] Galatians 2:20

The Christians who are romantically involved with non-Christians, show that pleasing God are not relevant to their personal desires.

4. **Are wiser than God.**

The Christians who engages sentimentally with unbelievers, demonstrate that they believe they are wiser and smarter than God. When the Lord speaks by giving prohibitions, counsel and exhortations, He draws from His Wisdom; and when the youth choose not to obey these commands but to rely on their own prudence, they make less the wisdom of God consequently they disparage the wisdom of God. It shows that they give more value their wisdom than to God's; they think they are wiser than God.

In addition, the Christians who engage with unbelievers, show that they believe that their convictions will protect them more than the counsel of God's Word. When God speaks, He does so for the protection of the same believers, because He knows what is best for Christians and what is not. For example, not uniting unequally with unbelievers protects the believers from the risks of run away from the Lord's ways, because is more probably the unbelievers affect their life negatively than positively. Leaning on their own opinion rather than on the counsel of God, show that the Christians have more confidence in their convictions than in the Word of God.

5. **Have preference for the world's children than God's children**

Christians who engage in a loving relationship with non-believers rather than with one of their own people demonstrate that they have preference for the devil's children over the God's children. that is, it shows that, their interest in the members of their own people is less than for the members of alien people who do not consider the affairs of God.

The Lord exhorts in His Word to give preference to one another among Christians.[42] The Christians who prefer to join sentimentally to unconverted one, prove that they have not considered to obey this exhortation of the Lord.

Praying for Wisdom

Following with the actions to choose wisely, the Christians should pray to choose the person who is appropriate as loving partner. In their usual prayer, the believers should ask for wisdom to choose whoever fulfills the essential qualities to be their ideal loving partner. When the wisdom misses are most likely to choose according to the will of man and not according to than God's will, that is why the prayer is key to receive from the Lord the precise guidance to make an excellent choice.

The Lord will respond to the prayer of the righteous who cries out for wisdom to choose their partner well.[43] The ears of Jehovah are attentive to the cry of the righteous to answer their requests. That is why it is good for youth to pray fervently when they are ready to choose a loving partner, so to receive from the Lord the precise orientation and thus choose according to His will. In His Word, the Lord has promised that, the one who asks, it shall be given; and the one who seeks, it shall find; and the one who knock, it shall have opened.[44] Then people must pray with faith to make an excellent choice, because there is a promise that He hears and answers the prayers.

Now, just as it is important to pray for, so it is also important to pay attention to the Lord's response to accept and obey it. If the

---

[42] Romans 12:10
[43] Psalms 34:15
[44] Matthew 7:7

response what is received from the Lord indicates that the person the Christians intend is not the best option, they must give up that intention, because otherwise they would be doing their will and not the will of God. And if they do not obey God's answer, then prayer was only a pretext.

To pray constantly for wisdom and to be attentive to the Lord's response will help youth to choose the person who, according to the will of God, will be the right for them.

To choose according to values and not according to physical attributes

To choose wisely, Christians must evaluate the person in election according to values and not according to physical attributes. Youth should learn to give more importance to the values what people in election possess than to physical attributes. For example, they should give more importance to, if the person is Christian to than if is pretty, they should also give more importance to, if the person is responsible and honest to than if the person has nice body. When the Christian chooses according to values, a life of peace is guaranteed even if the person chosen is not very physically attractive.

Today's society has guided youth to choose by giving more importance to physical appearance than to values. These demands have led youth to become more interested in maintaining a good physical appearance than to improving their principles and values of life. So that, today we see people with faces and bodies almost perfect but with a disordered life in most cases. However, believers should not act according to the demands of the world, they should not be carried away by the impression of a beautiful face or a toned body, because they are more likely to choose a person with whom they will hardly be happy. To be guided by appearances can be counterproductive for Christians, because grace and beauty are deceitful and fleeting,[45] while the values are permanent, and the more time passes, the more they are perfected.

---

[45] Proverbs 31:30

The Christians who choose according to values will be decided by a person who:

1. **Preferably is hardworking.**

   People who choose their loving partner according to values are regularly decided by a person who is hardworking. When people choose according to values, will evaluate if the person to choose has the virtue of being strenuous. In this case, the male will warn if the woman is honorable, extraordinary, strong, good housewife, industrious, efficient, prosperous and valuable; these are the characteristics that define a virtuous woman. The young women, on the other hand, will warn if the man is responsible, diligent, hardworking, protective, honest and all other good virtues which we may mention. And both will notice whether the other person has love for God and His work, whether is whole, whether has loyalty, whether is respectful, whether is generous, whether is tolerant, whether is responsible and kind.

   The value of being hardworking is an important characteristic to be evaluated by those who choose according to values. The Christians who want to have a hardworking person at their side should place aside the habit of choosing only according to physical attributes and focus on making a choice in which values are given much importance.

2. **Preferably does not have a compromising sexual past.**

   People who choose their loving partner according to the values are most likely to be decided by a person who has no compromising sexual past. People who have a committed sexual past are who have voluntarily lost their virginity, because they have been influenced by the idea that it has no value and that can have all the sexual experience they want and with whom want without being married. This excludes those people who have been victims of rape or any sexual abuse, because they are not to blame for the evil of others; and not excluding them would be unfair. Whoever chooses according to values, preferably choose a person who voluntarily decided to keep them self-pure and virgin for marriage. Such a person demonstrates that has a high sense of moral purity and has a high commitment to honorability. And by those principles, it is very likely that they will give a high value to the marriage and cling to the idea that it is forever. So, a Christian person who chooses the loving partner giving more importance to values than to physical attributes is very likely to be very happy in their relationship.

Now, my intention is not to induce Christians to completely rule out people with a compromising sexual past, nor to condemn marriages with people who have that issue, because we all deserve a second chance, and completely rule out who by mistake, had sexual experiences would be unfair; especially for those who are already believers. My purpose is to point out that, if Christians choose mates with a compromising sexual past, it could have consequences, which, if they do not know how to manage them, could seriously affect their courtship and marriage. For example. If a man decides to take a woman with children as his bride, he must be prepared to accept that, the relationship includes not only the relationship with those children, but also the tolerance of seeing the father of those children arrive at his girlfriend's house to interact with them. In the same way if a young lady gets involved with a divorced man and has children, she must be tolerant to the relationship of her boyfriend with his ex-wife based on those children. And since not all people are mature enough to cope with this kind of relationship, I advise that, it is preferable to choose a person without compromising sexual past and thus avoid later problems. Now, if the Christians believe they can manage and avoid the consequences I mentioned earlier, I only advise them to honor the chosen one as if they had found them virgin and to forget their past, so as not to make further claims. I express this, because when times of discord arrives, is usually that such complaints arise; because I have met women who after living with a male several years still receive complaints because the man did not find her virgin, I also know couples who are not happy, because one of the spouses does not relate well to the children who are not of both. And finally, I add the recommendation to require their partner to set clear rules as to the relationship with their former partner, so that it does not affect the new relationship. This includes regular visiting times, call schedules, visits made when they are present at home, etc. I conclude by reiterating that, if the Christians do not have enough maturity to support a relationship with a person who has a compromising sexual past, it is preferable to move forward with someone else who does not have it, because doing so will result in a bitter life for both and that is not fair.

On the other hand, choosing a person without compromising sexual past help the Christians to avoid the risk of yielding to the temptation of illicit sex. What you have not had, you do not need it, but what you have had and suddenly is taken away from you, you will long for it. This is the situation for people who have had sex experiences, it will be difficult for them to control their sexual desire, because sex is highly pleasurable and highly captivating, and because they already know what it comes after the kisses and the caresses. That is, since they are already accustomed to having sex, kisses and simple caresses do not satisfy them, therefore, they will give themselves the task of seeking their satisfaction. But if the

Christians believe that can control that risk, I only advise them to be very cautious and to avoid excessive physical contact at all costs, and if it is possible to avoid it completely, this will help them to remain pure and holy for the Lord.[46]

The person who chooses according to values will be inclined to a person without a committed sexual past or by a person committed to sexual purity, even if the latter has had a compromising sexual past, in the latter case, will be wise to control all risks and consequences.

Express the intentions to the person chosen

Once the person has been chosen, and after praying, it is up to the Christian male to make the declaration of his intentions. This statement must be made with much formality and security, just as Abraham's servant did to Rebekah's parents when he assigned him the task of seeking a wife for Isaac.[47] This is the key step of choosing loving partner process, all the steps revolve around this crucial moment, because is the step for what all the previous steps have been performed. That is why it must be planned in detail and be very careful not to waste everything that has been done.

Inform parents and spiritual leaders

Keeping abreast the parents is a step Christians must take before consummating courtship. After making his intentions known to the chosen girl and obviously obtaining the yes, the Christian man is obliged to appear before the young girl's parents and express to them his intention to enter a meaningful relationship with her, so that, they be the first to know about the new relationship. The boy must also present the girl to his parents so that they no longer see her as a friend, but as the future wife of their son.

---

[46] Proverbs 14:16
[47] Genesis 24:34-41

No young Christian should initiate the engagement relationship with a young lady, much less kiss or caress her without first talking to her parents and have the respective permission. In the world, youth are engaged in love affairs and the last to know out are the parents, but among Christians it should not be so, because that dishonors the parents. Each young man should remember that the first commandment with promise is to honor father and mother.[48]

The couple's spiritual leaders should also be informed of their intention to unite in a loving relationship. It is right for pastors and youth leaders to know about the relationships of their fellow servants, for they also will give account of their sheep to the Lord.[49] As they are their shepherds, they have the right to be informed about the sentimental affairs of their sheep, because part of the care towards their fellows includes giving the pertinent recommendations whatever the case.

Pray together asking for blessings

It is prudent for the new couple to take time to pray together prior to formalizing the courtship relationship. Having both consent and parental consent, it is recommended the couple to spend some time praying asking the Lord for a special blessing for the relationship. Praying together will help to create the habit of prayer as a couple and will serve as a foundation for doing so every day when they be already married. Praying together will strengthen friendship, courtship and future marriage.

I personally consider that six months is a prudent time to pray. During that time, it is good for the suitors to remain alone as friends, to get to know each other a little more and finally to discern whether the courtship relationship should be consummated.

The life of Christians is based on prayer, so it is important the couple create the valuable habit of praying together from the previous stage and during the courtship.

---

[48] Deuteronomy 5:16
[49] Hebrews 13:17

Reflection.

For God, the choice of couple within His People has always been and will be something that requires a lot of wisdom. So much so, that in biblical times, He delegated to parents the responsibility of deciding with whom the son was married and to whom the daughter was gave.[50] The parents were very careful in the accomplishment of this task, because the chosen person became part of their family, and what they wanted least was for their children to marry people who would stain the name of that family or to divert it in adoration of other gods, since, they knew that they would have to account to the Lord of it for being the unique responsible before Him.

Parents wisely chose their children's partner, because they were outside the influence of feelings. They focused on ensuring a stable and lasting marriage for their children; and to do so, they left aside all the vanities which could lead them to failure. They also focused on ensuring continuity of exclusive worship of the Name of God in their families, and for reach this, they excluded any person whose practices were pagan, no matter their physical appeal, their good social or economic status. It was not difficult for them to choose with the mind, because the influence of feelings was null, therefore, they chose wisely.

To choose a couple with the same wisdom as the parents in the people of Israel, it is advisable you to also leave the influence of the feelings and apply the same principles of wisdom which the parents applied in the choice process of the couple for their children. While it is true that this society has taught you that the heart is the one who commands and you must choose according to what your feelings dictate, it is also true that the heart is perverse and deceitful more than all things,[51] and if you choose guided by him, it is very likely that you will choose the person you would least like to share for the rest of your life. Now, if you choose wisely, leaving aside the vanities and superficialities that feelings generate, you are likely to choose the right person, and therefore have a stable and lasting relationship, and in which the Name of the Lord be glorified forever. Choose your partner with the mind and not with the heart.

---

[50] Deuteronomy 7:3
[51] Jeremiah 17:9

Currently in the societies is handled the idea that it is very necessary you to like the person to be chose to feel good and to make your engagement successfully. Through soap operas and love stories, society has been convinced by pre-established figures that liking is the basis of happiness in a loving relationship. And that concept has become so rooted in people that has even been adopted by many Christians, including leaders. My opinion on this is that, like is a "nice to have"; it is good if you have it, but if you do not have it, it does not affect you, because it is not important. The basis for my opinion is the Bible; because, in it we find many stories in which the couples were formed at the will of the parents without the consent of the children and then had stable and lasting marriages. Now, I'm not saying it's bad that you like the person to choose, I'm not saying that if you like the person to choose your courtship will be a failure. What I am trying to tell you is that, if you find a person whose qualities point to be your ideal partner, you should try to join him or her even if you do not like physically, because the most important thing is that your values fit with him or her own, because like will not be a comfort to you when you be during problems of infidelity or domestic violence or addictions or otherwise. To choose according to what the world proposes does not always give satisfactory results in the real life, only in the soap operas, but that is fiction. Give more importance to the values of people than to what you feel.

A great friend told me that youth should see marriage as a life project and courtship as the stage of pre-feasibility of that project. And I agree with his words, because if you take your courtship as such, the least you will care is whether someone likes you or not, but you will focus on finding the person who has the perfect qualities to be your ideal partner in marriage. That is, share your Christian vision, your family goals and your personal goals; to be your support in times of distress and to remain faithful to the purposes of marriage. All that comes down to making a choice with wisdom.

The Lord will please you if you choose your loving partner with the mind and consequently will make you fall in love with her. Doing so, He will bless your relationship to be prosperous, stable and lasting.

Chapter 6

Attitudes that Christians take to maintain their courtship in holiness

Living in holiness must be a premise for Christians during the courtship. One of the stages in which the holiness is exposed to risks is in the courtship, especially because the freedoms in the physical contact that society has allowed today. To minimize these risks and maintain a courtship worthy of Christians, the couple must place as principles of conduct the advice of the Word of God; because two Christians do not make a Christian courtship, if when they are interacting between them, they forget the principles of God and give free rein to their passions. It becomes necessary then, they fear God and apply His Word to live a courtship in holiness. In other words, as good doers of the Word,[52] they have to practice each commandment and take every warning of the Lord seriously, because only the knowledge of the Word is not enough to live in holiness but is necessary to place it as a fundamental norm of conduct and as a guide to every act of life.

---

[52] James 1:22

For a courtship to be a Christian, it must fulfill the premise of keeping the couple in holiness, therefore, those involved must strive to have their courtship perform the following behavioral actions:

Do not idolize the couple53

In a courtship relationship, Christians do not idolize the couple. It is often the case that, youth get so excited about courtship and because of it, they give more importance to strengthening that relationship than relationship with God. In those cases, both lose the perspective of what God must mean for them, and they remove from their agendas all activities related to God which overlap with their dates. The time they used to pray and read the Bible or to attend the congregation, now they occupy it for their romantic moments. All their personal activities are confined to take care of courtship and, therefore, neglect their relationship with the Lord. That shows that they love the loving partner more than the Lord. They forget that to love another being before God is idolatry and those who do such a thing are not worthy of the Lord. [54]

Neglecting the relationship with the Lord to strengthen the courtship relationship can bring negative consequences to the life of the couple, of which I will mention some below:

1. **To clash with sin.**

   One of the consequences that idolatry generates is crashing into sin by yielding to temptation. The risk of crashing increases as one or both members of the couple are carnal; that is, the more they neglect their relationship with God, weaker spiritually they will be; and the more weakness they have, the more carnal they will be; and the more carnal they are, greater will be the risk of yielding to temptation and committing to sin. Christian couples who neglect their

---

[53] Mathew 10:37
[54] Mathew 10:37

relationship with God to strengthen theirs, usually become vulnerable to temptations by increasing the risk of yielding to them.

To avoid such a consequence, the bride and groom should be wise and correct that kind of attitude by seeking to resume all their devotional activities regularly to strengthen their spiritual life.

2. **Manipulation.**

Another of the consequences the idolatry leaves is the manipulation which exercises the idolized one to whom idolizes. This happens because, who idolizes makes his life turn completely around the idolized one, and this pushes the idolized to take control, not only of the relationship, but also of the actions and thoughts of whom idolizes, manipulating what he wishes. Such a relationship like this is very dangerous, because it gives the opportunity to the idolized one to do what he wants without being aware of the consequences that involve those acts. Those who idolize their partner are exposed to being dragged by the ideas of their lover including good and bad.

Another way in which manipulation is manifested is when the bridegroom exercises over the bride the authority which only the parents have the right to exercise over her. This happens when the bridegroom restricts schedules and controls the activities of the bride, to the extent that, she must ask permission to perform those activities even though she already has the consent of their parents. Such an attitude is detrimental to the couple and a lack of respect for the bride's parents, because, although it is true that the Lord has delegated the authority of the couple to the man, it only applies exclusively in marriage, not in courtship. Therefore, the bride who idolizes her boyfriend, is exposed to sin of injustice allowing her boyfriend to usurp the authority which only the parents can exert on her.

To avoid this kind of consequences, the couple must place the Lord at the center of their relationship, in that way, their courtship will be in accordance with Christian practices.

3. **Emotional instability.**

Another of the consequences of idolizing the couple is to fall into emotional instability when the relationship ends without marriage. This happens because the idolaters feel that their life do not make sense if the other person is not by their side. That can be very critical, because, the affected person may think that it is impossible to live without the loving partner, and in those circumstances, they could think that suicide be a viable option to escape the problem. Then, whoever idolize their partner are exposed to emotional instability and grave consequences.

To correct this type of attitude, the couple must avoid idolatry by remembering that no one, except God, is indispensable to live unless their vital organs are connected to the loved one.

To have a courtship as suited to saints, the couple must be careful not to displace God from the priority He deserve. The bride and groom must stand firm in the good practices of faith, trying not to lower their frequency in prayer, in reading the Bible and attendance the devotional services of the congregation. For that, they should plan their dating at times which do not overlap with those activities which are crucial to the growth of their spiritual life. By doing so, they will avoid idolatry and reduce risks.

Flee from Fornication[55]

In courtship relationship, Christians must have a recurrent task of fleeing from fornication. Youth must take steps of wisdom to prevent being seduced by sin. Among these measures they have:

1. **To reject the liberties which the world gives to the courtship.**

   To escape from fornication and maintain a relationship of courtship in holiness, it is necessary for young Christians to reject all the freedoms which society gives to courtship today. The worldly idea that the more intimate, the more effective courtship will be; and the more sexually involved, the better guarantee to be together for ever is, it should not be for Christians. Because this idea promotes practices which should be abhorrent to them, since it makes permissible sexual intercourse without marriage, which goes against the desire to live in holiness. That is the reason why, since the beginning of the relationship, it is up to the couple to withdraw from their minds the idea that they have an open license to intimate, using as pretext to live together as if they were husbands to see if the relationship works; it does not apply to Christians, because it is sin.

2. **Be sober especially in the dates.** [56]

   To escape from fornication and maintain courtship in holiness, young Christians must keep their hearts sober during the dates. It is in dates where the risks of giving in to temptation are maximized, and those risks increase the probabilities to lose the judgment. That is why youth should try, for those moments, to have a healthy mind; to be sensible, reasonable, prudent, judicious and have self-control.

---

[55] 1 Corinthians 6:18
[56] Titus 2:6

To achieve the purpose of staying sober in the dates, boyfriends should know, which in my view, is the curve of temptation control.

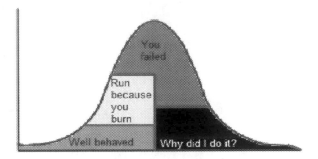

The first zone of the curve marks the area in which emotions can be easily controlled. I called to that area " Well Behaved "; it is in that area where the bride and groom should try to stay the whole date.

The second zone marks the negotiation that the temptation begins with the couple to convince them to sin. I call this area "Run because you burn". In this area, the couple has partially controlled emotions, because the thoughts are beginning to cloud, so that the instinct begins to want to take control of the acts. It is coming to that area when the bride and groom should be wise and cancel the date for another day, this must be to avoid the danger.

The third zone marks the moment when concupiscence gives birth to sin, because the couple has completely lost control of their emotions and yielded to the temptation. I call this area "You failed, you have sin". This is the area in which couples should avoid falling, because it is in which emotion has complete control over reasoning and instinct over wisdom. In that situation, the bride and groom make any mistakes.

And finally, the fourth zone is the one that marks the moment when the control over the emotions is regained, however, it is already late, because it happened what should not have happened. I call this area "Why did I do it?". In this area there is remorse, complaints and tears. However, it is only as an outlet, because unfortunately they were not wise to prevent error.

To maintain a courtship worthy of being called a Christian, fiancés must try tirelessly to keep themselves sober, because, only by maintaining control over their instincts, they will maintain their courtship in holiness.

3. **Avoid excessive physical contact.** [57]

To minimize the risk of yielding in to temptation and to live a courtship in holiness, it is necessary for youth to avoid excessive physical contact during their dates. No Christian bride and groom plan to give up in to temptation and have premarital sex, but when the time passes, the right conditions are gradually being created and one day it happens. Excessive physical contact accelerates the creation of those conditions; caresses for extended periods prepare the body for sexual intercourse; and once, they are in that condition, they are more vulnerable to yield to the temptation. That is the reason why it is very important to Christian couples to avoid at all cost's excesses in the corporal frictions, because this will help them not to expose themselves to sin. Understanding by excessive physical contact to any stimulus which alters the normal state of the body and increases the desire to have sex.

Knowledge of the instinctive reactions of the body will help youth to be wise and avoid excessive physical contact. Something that the couple must consider, is that the

[57] Ecclesiastes 1:18

human body gradually increases the limit of satisfaction to any experience. For example, at the beginning of the relationship, holding hands and giving simple kisses satisfies the expectations of the couple, but as time goes on, the body goes up the limit of satisfaction and it becomes necessary to add more heat to the kisses and caresses to feel satisfied; and in proportion as the limit of satisfaction rises, so does the tone of physical contact, until the sexual relationship becomes necessary to feel satisfied. The wisdom manifested in avoiding too much body interaction will help the couple not to yield to the temptation.

In the courtship among Christians, holiness is so important that if it is necessary to maintain a complete avoidance of physical contact, it must be done. I know the story of a couple of boyfriends who had to choose to live their courtship without kisses and without caresses, because both had had sexual experiences before meeting and being Christians; and as they knew their limits, they decided not to have physical contact during their courtship to avoid being exposed to the temptation. That is the kind of attitude which Christian boyfriends must take to demonstrate they are very committed to holiness.

Moderating the physical contact in dates and controlling the increase of the limits of satisfaction will help youth to flee from fornication and to keep living in the holiness which our God demands from His children.

4. **Avoid dating in private places.** [58]

A courtship between Christians requires very clear rules to fulfill, in order to facilitate the escape of the temptation and maintain in holiness the relationship. One of those

---

[58] Proverbs 9:17

basic rules is not have dates in lonely, isolated or dark places. Dating in very private places expose the couple to the risk of sinning, because they foster intimacy; and the less exposed they are to risk, the less chance they will have to be tempted. For this reason, it is advisable for the couple to arrange their dates in places where do not provoke to go beyond the kisses. For example, it is not convenient for them to have their appointments at friends' houses or at the girl's house when she is alone; or in her bedroom, even if the parents are at home, or in any other place that fosters an intimate environment. They should also be careful not to have their dates late in the night without the supervision of parents or an older adult, especially for the holidays.

Avoiding dating in solitary and isolated places is an effective way to escape from fornication and favor a courtship in holiness.

5. **Do not dress provocatively.** [59]

Another rule that Christian couples should keep in mind to flee fornication and to facilitate a courtship in holiness is that the woman avoids dressing provocatively for dating. The clothing we wear sends unconscious messages to the people around us and further reflects the personality, character, intentions and judgment of a person. Dressing provocatively causes the woman to unconsciously send a sexually suggestive message to the male, who will receive it by his sexual stimulus point; which is the sense of sight; and this will awaken in him the desire to have sex. And since man by nature is a hunter and any stimulus can increase his ability to hunt, it is very likely that he tries to satisfy his instinct, trying to consummate the sexual act. So, to minimize visual provocation to her loving partner, it is good

---

[59] 1 Timothy 2:9

young girls not to wear provocative clothes in their dates, but the one that is in perfect harmony with their profession of faith. For a woman who loves Jesus Christ will try not to provoke with her clothes, because her main interest will be to show the character of God in everything she does and in everything she wears. If a woman dresses as a Christian should dress, her dress will reveal purity and chastity, she will not be interested in showing her body to compete with others, or to stimulate the sight of her boyfriend.

To avoid dressing provocatively young girls must be firm in the foundations of the Christian faith. This I express, because, unfortunately, these days we are living in a society highly hedonistic and obsessed with physical appearance and fashion, which causes; in most cases; that men see women more as a sexual object than as a woman to form a family. This is because designers today have eroticized fashion by promoting styles that suggest sex everywhere. These styles are characterized by promoting the use of extremely tight or extremely short clothes or dresses with pronounced necklines or blouses and transparent skirts or super tight pants that leave nothing to the imagination. To avoid the use of this kind of clothing, the young women must fight against the practices of society that presses them to follow all this mundane current of the fashion; and for this, they must be very firm in the biblical principle which teaches that the woman should dress with decorum, modesty,[60] looking for the way not to attract the men eyes to her body dressing emphasizing her physical attributes, but emphasizing the spiritual virtues that adorn her.

To avoid the sin of fornication in Christian courtship, a woman must avoid dressing provocatively. She should wear clothing that reflects honor, decency, purity, honesty,

---

[60] 1 Timothy 2:9

modesty, and chastity, on the contrary she will awake in her boyfriend the natural desire to have sex.

6. **Clear the mind of all sexual contamination.** [61]

To escape from fornication and live in holiness during courtship, Christians must seek to cleanse themselves all things that can contaminate their minds with sex. The Christian testimony contains one of the highest values that must do with the definitive elimination of everything that represents sexual dirt inside their life. Because the Holy Spirit dwelling in them, their responsibility is circumscribed to take from them all the old leaven (sin) that corrupts their life.[62] Therefore, the effort to cleanse their life of all contamination of sexual sin is mandatory.[63]

To flee from sin, Christian boyfriends must wipe their minds from the pollution that pornography creates. Pornography is an evil that has become widespread, which is affecting the mind and spirit of many young Christians and non-Christians today; and has become so deeply rooted in society that it is affecting even the leaders of Christian congregations. It is the task of youth to close the doors of their minds and hearts to this terrible evil that is causing pollution to many Christians using technology as a highway to expand their venom.

The technology has violated the privacy of many believers by facilitating access to sexually explicit videos, magazines and photographs. Before, who wanted to see pornography, had to take the public step of buying a magazine or to go to a movie theater. That public step was enough to restrict

---

[61] 2 Corinthians 7:1
[62] 1 Corinthians 5:6
[63] 1 Corinthians 5:7

access and to be fascinated with it, because not everyone was encouraged to pass the shame of being identified with that hobby. Now, with the appearance of the Internet, the barrier of this public step disappeared as well, making accessible all the obscene material, within reach of a single Click. That easiness has led eight out of ten young men with Internet access to have had some visual experience with images of nudity and explicit sex; has also led to every second, 3,075.64 users are going through a pornographic site; that every second 28,258 Internet users are exposed to pornographic images; that every second, 372 Internet users are writing adult terms on the search engines and that every 39 minutes, a new pornographic video is being created in the United States.[64] [64] It is alarming then, as this evil has infected our youth and adults, both women and men. It is against all this siege that youth must fight to rid their minds of the sexual contamination that pornography generates. To do this, they must be brave and courageous, so as not to be part of the great crowds affected by this terrible and destructive evil.

When the guys clean their mind of the sexual contamination, Christian bride and groom will get rid of several consequences that causes this evil: First, they will get rid of seeing their partner as an object to satisfy their sexual whims. Secondly, they will minimize the risk of giving up in to the temptation to fornicate, because with one of both has a contaminated mind, it becomes very easy to give in it, so that the priority of the affected will be to seek the opportunity to satiate their sexual desires as soon as possible without measuring the consequences. Thirdly, they will get rid of the dreams and plans that every young person has, because of pornography, there are many youths who have not reached their dreams, because they were married prematurely and forced to assume the consequences of their actions. And

---

[64] Top ten reviews – Internet pornography statistics

fourth, they will get rid of sinning against the life of a baby, because of pornography, there are many young women who have decided to have an abortion, due to the lack of support from the couple and the parents. As seen, the consequences of pornography are harmful to the holy life which God requires of His children. For this reason, youth must fight with all their strength to get rid of the mental and spiritual contamination that this evil generates to those who fall into it jaws.

7. Keeping clean from sexual contamination will help Christian couples to flee from the sin of fornication and therefore to live a courtship in holiness. Isolating themselves wisely from all contact with sexually explicit material is imperative. If they do so, they will get rid of many problems.

Reflection.

All Christians are characterized by being holy in their way of life, because they do not adapt to the thoughts of the world, but heeds God's call to be like the one who called him.[65] The priority of the believers are to walk in righteousness always, because their mind warn of the constant presence of the Lord who is Holy, Holy, Holy and that makes holiness become their banner wherever they go and in any area in which they develop.

For the true Christians, living in holiness in all areas of their life are not negotiable, for their thinking is continually to be perfected in justice and truth; so that every day that passes, they be more holy,[66] although the world around them are increasingly lost in evil.

On the basis of the above, I tell you that if you are a Christian, all immorality and impurity should not be part of your dating relationship.[67] Sobriety and temperance should be your faithful companions. Sobriety will help you keep control over your emotions and temperance will keep

---

[65] 1 Peter 1:14-16
[66] Proverbs 4:18
[67] Ephesians 5:3

you invariable in the face of temptations. If you do this, you will be guaranteeing a courtship worthy of being called Christian and very different from what the world promotes.

Although the people around you have engaged in courtship relationships in accordance with worldly customs, and they pressure you to do the same; you should try to add as much holiness as possible to your own, so that the Lord may be honored by your way of proceeding. The world will pressure you directly or indirectly to act according to their customs, and will try to make you think that excessive intimacy between couples is normal and helps to strengthen the relationship; at the same time, you will be qualified as a retrograde person if you decide to live it pure and holy. When that happens, you should remember that the darkness does not prevail in the light, because the light is so strong than it. You are the light of the world,[68] therefore the darkness of the world cannot place out your light. That means that, with a strong character, you must oppose the influence of those worldly thoughts, so that, your holy courtship be an effort that enlightens men and glorifies the Lord by your good testimony.[69] You are required then, do not let the pressures of this world dominate you and lead you to live a sinful courtship.

As an obedient son of God, try not to mold your courtship to the bad practices that the world has. Rather, try to live a courtship in holiness, because the one who called you said, "Be Holy because I am Holy".[70]

---

[68] Mathew 5:14
[69] Mathew 5:16
[70] 1 Peter 1:16

Chapter 7

Qualities which Christians add to their courtship to make it successful

A successful engagement is one that meets the established requirements and necessary conditions for what was created. This type of courtship is very clear that marriage is its main goal.

Every good Christian should strive to have a successful engagement. As far as they can, the Christians must do everything possible so that, their courtship fulfills the purpose for which it was created. We have said, on repeated occasions, that in the world people indulge in courtship only to satisfy their instincts; the tingling they feel in their stomach when they see the person, they like is the only reason why they get a loving relationship without worrying about giving a definite course to that relationship. What interests them is having fun, enjoying the company of the opposite sex and nothing else. However, the Christians do not have to follow that behavior, because they have been called to live by glorifying God with their deeds. Conscious of this role, the Christians should try to do everything possible to have a successful engagement.

To make courtship successful, care must be taken to add some qualities that I mention below.

Focus on the main objective

Courtship among Christians must focus on the main purpose of marriage. We have repeatedly mentioned that, in its primary conception, courtship is the stage of preparation for marriage. None truly Christian then should have a relationship of this kind unless to plan to get married.

Focusing on marriage will help the couple to maintain a well-defined north about the expectations of the relationship. All efforts should be aimed at achieving a happy marriage.

Focusing on the main purpose of courtship has two key goals:

1. **Schedule the date of the wedding.**

    Schedule the date of the wedding is an important goal to fulfill for a courtship to be successful. It is very well that, since the first months of the relationship, the bride and groom schedule an estimated date for the wedding ceremony. Doing this will have a well-defined north and a special goal to work with. My recommendation in this regard is that, in the first two months of the relationship, the couple should establish the year in which the ceremony will be held. Then, as the months go by, I recommend scheduling the month, this should not exceed the sixth month. And lastly, I recommend scheduling the day of the ceremony, so that, by the end of the first year of engagement, the date of the wedding is already scheduled, no matter if it will be one or more years later.

    However, if the frequency of dates is high, it is advisable that the wedding date be planned for one year at the latest, that is, the more frequent the dates, the closer the wedding date should be.

Scheduling the date of the wedding is a step of formality that adds success to the courtship relationship. It is good to schedule the date of the marriage from the beginning of the relationship, so that, the couple concentrates on the preparation for that magnificent event and all the other responsibilities it entails for the rest of their lives. A courtship with established wedding date is a formal and successful relationship.

2. **Saving money to make the initial capital for the future marriage.**

It is recommended to couple to save money in order to make the initial capital for the future marriage. If both works, it is good that they agree and define how much money of their monthly earnings will save for down payment of the house, for purchase the furniture and for expenses for the wedding ceremony. Every marriage needs a capital to function well, therefore, savings will help the couple to meet this goal.

Savings will help grooms to prevent economic problems in future marriage. Good savings will help the couple to prevent future disagreement discussions due to a lack of money to meet food, clothing and roof needs. The bride and groom should realize that, no matter how much love they have, lack of money can affect their future marriage. That is why, they must prepare economically during the courtship to reduce the chances of suffering.

Saving money to make the initial capital for the future marriage is a goal that the couple must handle with priority and seriousness. Because fulfilling it adds formality to the relationship, focuses courtship on its main goal and helps prevent future economic problems. In conclusion, meeting the goal of saving to make the initial capital of marriage, is a crucial step to the success of courtship.

Define aspects of the functioning for the future family

Additional to focus on the main objective, it is recommended the couple also to define some fundamental aspects on which the future family will be living.

1) **Aspects related to Faith**

   a) **Define the course of their future devotional life.**

   It is recommended the bride and groom to define the course of their devotional life when they be already married. A good devotional life will help them to strengthen their relationship with God and to improve their future marriage. That is why they should define the time and frequency of family and personal devotions.

   b) **Choose the church they will be congregated in.**

   It is good for the bride and groom to choose the congregation they will congregate in as active members once they be married. In case they congregate in different congregations during the courtship, it will be good they agree to decide which of the two to attend; it is advisable they to make that decision before the wedding, so that, both be very clear to which congregation they will attend, and to assure that it will not be a cause of discussion when they be already married.

   If the bride and groom attend different congregations, it is preferable for the woman to join the congregation where the man goes; this, because authority matter's, due to male has been called to be the head of woman[71] and she to hold on to authority to the husband.[72] However, if the congregation where the bride goes has doctrinal practices better grounded in the correct interpretation of the Bible, it is better they to congregate there.

If it is necessary to choose another congregation for the purpose of domicile, I recommend that, the election be done with great care, because in recent times apostasy is reigning in the doctrinal practices of many congregations, which have departed from good doctrine to follow what the apostle Paul called doctrines of demons.[73] In this case, it is advisable to seek a congregation whose practices be based on the correct interpretation of the Bible.

In conclusion, choosing the congregation to attend when they be already married is a strong key step the couple must to give in order to have successful courtship. They should never decide to attend different congregations. It does not work!

c) **Define the level of commitment in the Ministry.**

It is good that the bridegrooms define in advance the level of participation they will have in the Ministry of Faith when they be already married. This will help them to build their future weekly agenda on which to base their active participation in the church to which they congregate.

---

[71] 1 Corinthians 11:33
[72] 1 Peter 3:1
[73] 1 Timothy 4:1

Preparing the agenda, they should well-balance the responsibilities of the congregation with household chores. A good balance will help to avoid frequent complaints from spouses about the neglect of household responsibilities by one of them. Because it is recurrent to listen to women complaining that husbands do not devote enough time to attend family because the congregation's affairs, or to men complaining that wives do not adequately attend to housework because they are engaged in the affairs of the congregation. A well-balanced agenda will help not neglect either the activities of the congregation or the commitments of the home.

In conclusion, the definition of the level of commitment in the Ministry of Faith they will have, is important because it will help the bride and groom to prevent nonconformities by neglecting future responsibilities and help them to project the treasures they will make in heaven, backed by quality of service they will give to the Lord when they be already married.

2) **Aspects related to the administration of the home**

a) **Define whether one or both will work for income.**

During the courtship stage, it is good for the couple to define whether one or both will work to raise funds for the future family. This will help them gain insight into what their economy will look like in the early years of marriage.

The best economic model for Christian marriage, is in which the man works to bring daily sustenance to the family and the woman fulfills the duties of motherhood, which consist in giving birth to children and making them grow, taking care of them and transmitting them the good values, so that, they be Christians of good testimony.[74] Now, I know that, in our societies, where women have reached spheres that had denied them in the past, is not easy for them to accept this advice. However, when a woman chooses to work outside the home, she automatically leaves the responsibility for duties of motherhood to kindergarten or to grandparents or to the domestic service worker or other third parties. These third people are those who end up educating the children, transmitting their values; which, many times, are not according to what is expected. For in most cases, kindergarten centers do not have a personalized attention for children; by other side, grandparents are usually very permissive or pimps with grandchildren; and the domestic service worker will not regularly educate with the love that a mother does, because nobody else will do the motherhood duties well like mothers do. Consequently, many of the children of these kind of marriages grow up without good spiritual guidance, and, in most cases, when they reach the youth age, they become with a rebellious character due to the lack of maternal presence. It is to be expected, then, that if the woman leaves the privilege of being the mother to go to work outside the home, her children will most likely not grow up with the good Christian values the couple had planned for them. If the priority of future marriage is that their children grow based on Christian principles, it is advisable to define adopting the model in which the husband works, and the wife attends to the duties

---

[74] 1 Timothy 2:15

of motherhood. And in case that; due to economic scarcity the woman needs to work, to do it in a homemade way or to set up her own business or in a part-time job is the best decision she may take. The idea is she works staying close to their children long time in day; so that, she may contribute to the family without neglecting the maternal responsibilities.

For engagement to be successful, it is important for the couple to have defined what economic model they will adopt to obtain the monetary income for survival of the future marriage.

b) **Define whether they will plan the number of children to have.**

Courtship is a good stage for the couple to define whether to plan the number of children to have in the future marriage. Establishing a position as to whether they will use any planning method is important; because depending on that decision, the couple must act, either to prevent and space pregnancies or to prepare to receive the children that God allows them to have.

In my opinion; unless the medical conditions of one or both does not allow it; it would be good for the couple to choose not to use planning methods and have the children God wants to give them. I know that in the XXI century and with all the advances of preventive medicine, this advice sounds controversial and retrograde. However, my rationale for doing so is as follows:

i. **There is no biblical argument to support family planning.**

Throughout the Bible there is not a single verse which serves as an argument to support man's authority to control pregnancies by spacing or preventing them. The term commonly used among Christians to justify the use of pregnancy prevention methods is "Wisdom" and the argument is that "it is wise to plan the number of children in order to give them a decent quality of life, considering how difficult is the economic situation and overpopulation in this stage that we are living". Now, if we speak about human wisdom, the argument is valid; because, in the middle of a society where the unemployment rate is high, wages are relatively low compared to the basic basket and access to health facilities is limited; the idea of having many children sounds crazy. However, if we speak of Divine wisdom, the argument loses all sense; because for the Lord, regardless of the economic situation of a country or location, the fruit of the womb continues to be a thing of high esteem and the one that fills of children in the youth, continues being extremely happy.[75] And as the Christian is called to conduct himself, not according to human wisdom but according to Divine wisdom (which among other things means to conduct himself in every circumstance according to the will of God, applying to his life the knowledge of His Word, knowing that He is present always and places), family planning should be

---

[75] Psalms 127:3-5

considered as the last option for Christians, whatever method is used.

ii. **For God, children are a blessing.**

The children whom the Lord gives are a blessing to those who receive them.[76] Children are a blessing from God to the parents. This was the feeling of the generations of biblical history and still in part of our times, because having many children was perceived as a great blessing, and not having them, was a source of shame, especially for women.[77] But unfortunately, now the practices have been reversed, because even among Christians, having many children is almost cause for shame and taunts, and having few is perceived as a great blessing and as a wisdom decision. Now, if children are a blessing for God, they should also be a blessing for Christians, because we should think just like Him.[78]

iii. **The children of the righteous do not beg for bread.**

In the Bible is written the promise that the children of the righteous do not beg for bread.[79] That promise guarantees God's care for the offspring of those who have been justified by faith in Jesus Christ. That means that the Lord provides daily sustenance to

---

[76] Psalms 127:3-5
[77] 1 Samuel 1:6
[78] 1 Corinthians 2:16
[79] Psalms 37:25

the seed of the righteous even during the worst global or local economic crisis. He does not need our help to keep His promise, because He is Almighty.[80]

The concern to satisfy the basic needs of the home is the main cause by which the couples venture to use a family prevention method, to limit the number of children. That concern makes sense when the hope of our future lies in our human capacities. However, when that hope lies in the Power of God, all concern loses meaning, because it is when we understand that the same God who provided the miraculous widow of Zarephath[81] during a great economic crisis, is the same God in which we have place our faith. And it is also the same God who, when lacked sustenance, miraculously fed five thousand men with only five loaves and two fishes.[82] I could continue listing biblical examples, however, I conclude that, whatever the economic situation of our society, Christians should not care for the daily sustenance of their children, to such a degree to make the decision to limit the number of them, because of that sustenance; for if the Lord feeds the birds of the field, which they sow not, neither do they reap; and He clothed the flowers of the field with splendor which did not weave, nor spin.[83] He will also provide food, clothing and a roof to

[80] Genesis 17:1
[81] 1 Kings 17:8-24
[82] Mathew 14:13-21
[83] Mathew 6:25-31

the seed of everyone who is of faith in Jesus Christ.

To conclude, whatever the decision that the couple takes as to whether to plan the number of children or not, it is important to do it in the stage of courtship. This will add formality to the relationship and makes courtship a successful relationship.

Reflection.

Every Christian has the responsibility to think in everything that gives good name and everything in which there is moral excellence and praise for these thoughts to become actions that glorify God.[84] As thoughts normally become actions, you as a Christian have the responsibility to think about having a formal engagement so that your actions lead you to materialize a successful courtship relationship.

Conceive in your mind the idea that your courtship will focus on achieving its main goal. Imagine that you arrive at a dock to board a boat, because you want to travel to a specific destination; and when you ask the captain, where is the destination port of the next trip; he replies that the boat is beautiful, that has the best comfort, with the latest technology, but he does not know where it is headed. Would you get on that boat? I'm sure not, because as much luxury as it has, what interests you is to reach the destination you have planned, and that boat would not be a resource can help you to make your trip successful. In the same way that, a sensible person would not conceive the idea of getting on a boat like the previous example, so a sensible Christian should not think of getting involved in a love relationship that does not have as main objective the marriage and nor have a direction traced to ensure the success of it.

Do not let the enemy undermine your mind by making you to believe that having formal courtship is only for people of the past or other times. Satan has poisoned culture and through it has taken captive the thoughts

---

[84] Philippians 4:8-9

of society to act according to his proposals. He has undermined the minds of youth with the idea that formality is a matter of old people and acting according to all good is only for retrograde people. Because of this, it is very likely that your friends pressure you to conceive in your mind the idea of having an informal courtship. They will tell you that you are not up to date, or you look old, or your thoughts are of old people, etc. When that happens, remember that, the Lord calls you to think different than the people who are in not Christians, acting different from them. For if the world thinks and acts according to the will of its prince, Christians think and act according to the will of the Lord, because we have the mind of Christ.[85]

I conclude this reflection by telling you that, it is imperative that you conceive in your mind the idea of having a formal courtship, so that, when be appropriate, you live a formal engagement. The role of the mind in the conception of your courtship is important, because you are what your thoughts are, and if you think of everything that is good name and in all there is moral excellence and praise, your courtship will be formal and successful.

I yearn with all my heart, that, today you take with courage and commitment the FIRM DECISION to have a courtship that honors God, your family and your future children.

---

[85] 1 Corinthians 2:16

About the Author

The author has been teaching about christian courtship for more than ten years while has been developmented his ministry as youth pastor in Evangelical Central American Church "Mies" in Puerto Barrios, Guatemala C.A.

The main interest for him is to teach values which young people could apply to their lives to be able to succeed in sentimental relationships.

Printed in the United States
By Bookmasters